WHORLED

WHORLED

POEMS

ED BOK LEE

COFFEE HOUSE PRESS

MINNEAPOLIS 2011

Coffee House Press books are available to the trade through our primary distributor, Consortium Book Sales & Distribution, www.cbsd.com or (800) 283-3572. For personal orders, catalogs, or other information, write to: info@coffeehousepress.org.

Coffee House Press is a nonprofit literary publishing house. Support from private foundations, corporate giving programs, government programs, and generous individuals helps make the publication of our books possible. We gratefully acknowledge their support in detail in the back of this book. To you and our many readers around the world, we send our thanks for your continuing support.

Good books are brewing at www.coffeehousepress.org

LIBRARY OF CONGRESS CATALOGING-IN-PUBLICATION DATA
Lee, Ed-Bok
Whorled : poems / by Ed Bok Lee.
p. cm.
ISBN 978-1-56689-278-0 (alk. paper)
I. Title.
PS3612. E34277W47 2011
811´.6—DC22
2011019754

Printed in the United States
5 7 9 8 6

ACKNOWLEDGMENTS
The following journals and anthologies first published work in this collection, sometimes in earlier versions. Much gratitude to these publications and the people associated with them: *Cimarron Review, MiPOesias, Softblow, KoreAm Journal, Hyphen, Mobius, An Uncertain Inheritance: Writers on Caring for Family* (HarperCollins, 2007), *Sleet, Great River Review, American Tensions: Literature of Social Justice* (New Village Press, 2011), *Asian American Literary Review, Spout, Taj Mahal Review, Dislocate,* and *Tinfish Review.*

Special thanks to my family and friends, to whom this book is dedicated—especially Oh Myo Kim, Sheila O'Conner, Ai, May Guillaume, David Mura, the Moledina-Wongs, the G.N. and Ball crews, Summit Fam, as well as to the McKnight Foundation and Martin Espada, the Loft Literary Center, the Joshua Tree Artists Residency, the Minnesota State Arts Board, the Ragdale Foundation, the New York Mills Artist Residency, the Anderson Center for Interdisciplinary Studies, and everyone at Coffee House Press.

for those who let love learn

Language is the only homeland.

—CZESLAW MILOSZ

[W]e continually find the First World in the Third,
the Third in the First, and the Second almost nowhere at all.

—HARDT AND NEGRI, Empire

What I am isn't important. Why is important.

—Old Boy, COMIC BY GARON TSUCHIYA AND
NOBUAKI MINEGISHI, FILM DIRECTED BY CHAN-WOOK PARK

1

2

3

4

1

All Love Is Immigrant

There is another other
in the other of every

Another

Heaven

An interview when I thought writing meant
articles, analyses, a lapidist's objectivity:
                                        Sunah
had been a Korean prostitute, come to America by way of rape,

drugs, abandon. Still, she possessed hope
at the core of the hoarsest human voice
that one day she would find a soft island of souls
overhandled like her own. Coolly, I asked

what the tattoo on her inner wrist said, before scarred
by an electric coil. "Flowers destroy their own stems," she exhaled
smoke. Sunah, 52, now just cleaned and cooked
ramen, Spam, and stir-fry for the illegal Asian women

rotated in every month en route to Arizona, California, New York.
This was on Lake Street in Minneapolis, next to
a strip-mall travel agency and Mexican bakery. Middle-
class men from the suburbs and migrant laborers

comprised most of their "massage" clients.
                                        Heaven, Sunah proclaimed,
was the working name of the undocumented sex worker
whose death I was covering. Lord

Jesus, I remember once I'd open my little arms,
heart, body genuflecting. Lately I overcontemplate
boys and their priests. Watch Native American women
stumble 3 a.m. streets. Think of Japan, Korea, Vietnam—a rice paddy

opening watery legs to a mortar shell, M-16 hail, each atom bomb's
orgasmic bouquet. Oily Mid-East needs. The finest
antebellum slaves. Wolves, unneutered dogs, the whole animal
kingdom.

I don't recall all Sunah rambled. But, unrelatedly,
sixteen months earlier, my girlfriend had become a cocktail
waitress at a high-end strip club downtown. I'd accused her of betraying
something sacred we shared, but couldn't find the naked-most word:

intimacy, culture, race—
                              I was scared and on unemployment . . .
Madam Sunah revealed little more of *Heaven*
than what the police report said.

Twice she wept, asking for a "little loan," then chuckled
at our doughnuts, my handwriting, the rain.
In the end, my article was a dressed-up skeleton:
Heaven had run, and her bosses, a Chinese and white couple

with private-school children, had sicced their thugs.
You can read about it in the paper.

They raped and blanketed the anonymous young woman with gasoline
and her spirit blossomed in secret like a history

no one would ever think is anything but a routine incineration near the city dump.
A funeral pyre whose black ink rising
I'll try to translate here for you now:

                              Motherfucker, let me in

Night Work

All summer, the city engine's low
roar capsizes our bodies into sleep,
groans,
        evacuation—
                    Lost to a watery
anamnesis so warm it requires a raft
thatched from death's
            flotsam to necklace its shore

        I swim on, calling your name

In my dreams, something is always deserting

But tonight, no fast shadows of birds
No oceanic flowers disrobing butterflies
or bright beach of child's porridge and bones—

                        Instead, someone weaving
a net from fallen hair in and around our bed
to catch the breath, blood, and ritual
motions that oiled us
            as one candle in a cave

In your dreams, someone is always resisting being saved

My teeth are on fire, you say I said

Don't fly for the labyrinth, once
I thought you were admonishing me to go away

I don't remember most others, a thousand seasons
phonographed in through a wounded window

Everyone can't have a cactus

Just o.k. empty all the rice from my legs

Once I awoke screaming, paws red-hot embers
You opened my mouth and poured a night-cold river in

Once you died and my heart fished all winter

Once we were eating lunch inside a kiln

Once you thought you smelled death,
but the lavender farm was too large to shave

On the fifth straight morning I'd dreamt of water
I stared at your face, its nacreous lids,
and I swear I could see a Glorious Ghost shifting
over your sun-warm waves

Water my birth sign, and one day my mother's death
that protect-fills my love with sadness

There, in words to my coworkers
it was still dripping, in my nods
over a galapagos of pages and forms

All love is immigrant, that autumn apparently
I mumbled

Your reply, after days: *Turn off the steam in the trees*

Somewhere right now, two lovers are conversing
without even knowing what their lives mean

One's heart gazelle-quick to survey a mountain his dead
        father is always vandalizing
The other frequently misplacing her hair, ears, or self-
sabotaging a crime

One usually struggling to stay alive
The other often untethering something

Or is it my mitochondria that powder-sugars the moon?
And you calcifying a promise inside to inscribe?

There is a dominion where inverses
invert until only terror, love, and imagination cling,

heavy, on human branches—enter your vista, phylum
unsequenced, dimmer deeds

Can you hear it tonight?
Wind in iron jars buried inside the living:
Grandmothers, past spouses, cable men, priests

Now! I finally manage
as our train smokes out all the rats on their bed of leaves

All night, I dive
down to the soft structures of some blue civilization's faith

In this myth of life, I keep forgetting whose ideas and
        sensations I'm supposed to be

Come morning: rain, trees, silvery
sleet
        and daily, this new fresh bounty
                we share, side by side

like angels coming home from work at a pearl factory

The Riddles

When I was six in Seoul,
Jimmy Riddle, son of an American
businessman, five-fingered
cash from my mother's purse
while hiding in our closet.

As the decades unfold
like a secret fist, I'm less
sure whose idea it was
to play hide-and-seek in the first place.

Stranded between admitting
Jimmy played me
and the possibility that I
set the kid up.

Experts say not until age seven
are children aware of race
and its consequences in psychological violence.
So maybe no cocky superiority
(complex) on his part. Maybe
I pitied the American.

Mrs. Riddle heavy with makeup
and highballs, always in a bathrobe.

Maybe in understanding some damage,
I longed to gift him the ₩ 17,000
as when I'd sometimes let my sister win at baduk.

Or, and this one improbably saintly—maybe I perceived
the need to teach him a lesson; to save my friend
from future, greater shame.

Mr. Riddle in sideburns like Reuben Kincaid
on *The Partridge Family*, nodding
in a three-piece suit when my mother
called a meeting in our kitchen
to discuss the theft, then threw
up her hand at the man's gold money clip—
That's not my point.

They'd been in-country a year,
which to a white family in the seventies
must have been like a luxury liner
broken ashore. Mr. Riddle
traded titanium and precious metals.
The few other American boys
I'd seen on smoky Seoul streets—feisty brown
halfies by u.s. servicemen.

Jimmy Riddle—pale, blond,
never came around again. I was forbidden
to traverse the alley to his concrete foreigners' compound.

Once a tiny Third World outpost, South Korea
now the globe's (and still u.s.-controlled) fifteenth-largest
        economic producer.
A lifetime later in America, I think
of Jimmy Riddle in certain moments—
random as our summer
of stickball, yakult, and screams.

There had to be
some other impulse, some reason
why
a rich white boy playing in a native's humbler apartment
would pocket cash
then deny, pretend, blame,

                        and never once cry—

Attention, yes; loneliness,
perhaps.
        Or here's another:
to shame his parents, maybe
even his race and nation—
some inverted perversion to belong.

Or am I just making excuses—
for all who manipulate,
cheat, lie, steal,
colonize?

Or is this all too easy?
Is the blinding dynamo here my own inner rationale—

Not only for Jimmy Riddle,
and his misplaced, dysfunctional family,
but also my own
                              small spun soul
tangled there, with his, somewhere
over that cold, inscrutable ocean?

She Means Poetry

Tŏl for body hair,
also meaning fur. *Shin*
mind, somewhere
amid head and heart.
English, all sinewy
wooden glisten falling
down stairs. *Pul,*
the grass I find you
sunbathing upon. Prisoner
of spears. I soldier
crawl so as not to disturb
the *sae*'s flying eyes over
your *tŏl*-less body.
Mal, the words
you almost utter
before. *Dal* is moon,
and also month.
Ddal, daughter.
Wŏl also month
and moon. History a
redundancy with
variation. *Nal* for the day
one of us will drift.
Bal, the feet enlisted

to stay. *Son,* a hand
directing reticence
or shots of *sul.*
Mal, speech, yes, but
also horse, slurred
or galloping at the *wŏl*
or *dal,* but never *ddal,*
unless ponytails
clutching a charred Bible.
Bul, fire. *Kal,* the knife
my grandmother
tucked in the past
century not just
to save her *pi,* but more
its rare silver handle.
Can you see me?
Like her I am
vainglorious
and fleeting. It matters
how I die as much
as what I do
to survive. An old
woman, who could
barely spell. Scratching
out *shi* after *shi* on (sweet
ssal) paper like me.
Arbitrary metaphors
repeatedly kissing

a twin sister bayoneted
off and drowned
for sedition in a
river's half-
frozen *mul*. Several
hundred art-
ifacts left for any
bird to decode.

Moon Projector Over Sea

The sea is the first
and oldest movie.

Life, the cluttered back-
stage of dreams.

In between, our
sleeping shadows
stealthily remove a single marionette
from the moon.

A human little
creature,

blind
as any star

shining
all afternoon.

Sweet Men

Atop their dresser mirror
rested a 2 x 4 my father used
to scratch his back

and discipline us. That
grained eye-knot
like a cougar in the bush.

Once I threw seaweed
into my sister's hair at lunch.
These were summers

of little-worth-remembering.
He hoisted my wrist
into the master bedroom

and whacked the dull backside
of my corduroys.
I never once thought

of my mother's pale skin
splashing against my darker father's;
how there where

my soul-sucking pleas and hands
went useless, they must have
sipped one another

many hot nights to sleep.
I do remember my mother
in his bathrobe once savoring a stringy persimmon

past midnight. Drips onto stainless
steel so slowly warped.
Her wet black hair never longer.

Years later, my lover's scent
layers my own: zephyr, cream,
dusk all summer.

I kiss her lids and take
her more deeply
in bed, cultivating

sorrow: part fear,
half prayer, waiting
for the moment

she begins to drown
so I can save her.
Some hot days

I'll rise afterwards
to the kitchen, craving
condensed milk and scalded coffee.

Musical ice cubes
in mugs for me and her.
As my father once

loved to sweeten
my own silly
tears.

How to Write Then Clone an Ethnic Poem

Scrape & breed
in a petri dish a swab

from your inner cheek
Love it as a stolen

mirror mists
Enunciate

Repeat another dream
Accept, over time,

if acceptable,
it will likely cringe

or simply shrug
at your odd expression

preserved in glass
Ignore the sign:

"Please do not eat"
upon entering

naked & clean
exhibit x

John Henry Tran (a.k.a. The Terminator)
vs. The System

I wanted to ask   what
happened to his hand—this Viet
first base new to our blackjack table.
We all did, I bet.

                     Chipped, flesh-
colored paint; such a dainty wood
prosthetic   screwed into what?

But in ten minutes flat dude dropped
$1,200 on a barbed chain of hits,
until homeboy on third finally says
Yo dawg, ain't no race;   Handless Man's
eyes now glassy—

                Down 13 grand,
he explained & shook
his head,   peeling five more c-notes
from a silver clip with his good hand's
feral fingertips.

                As we all   half-watched,
I looked around, wondering   why
past 3 a.m. in a sea of smoke,   death
bells & bubbly slot gurgles
is this damn prairie Indian casino

almost   all Asian—even
the dealers?

                              He will lose
$4,400 more. He will glare
each time harder at the waxen
Asian face that scoops
his shiny black stacks & junk.

Everyone will try not to stare
at his cheap toy of a hand (which,
incidentally, only once, while lighting
a Marlboro, did he wiggle to hit)—

the whole time,   wondering   not
what happened,   how
did he lose the real one—for in gambler's logic
that was perfectly clear
with supershit luck like his—but instead
why keep playing   here,
now, at this impossible
under sea hour,   senses
frayed,   you
sad, handless man
with something so obviously absent
why the hell   even try to pray?

Mnemonikos: A Foreigner's Figment

Every eye in this new land
a kind of jewel, wrote
Simonides of Ceos circa 500 BC
Full of dream, the young peasant

traveled by foot and boat for two years
to the ancient capital of Athens
in search of learning, art, and wisdom
One night, during a banquet of music and merriment,

King Sopas, bored with his fools and fire-eaters, stood drunkenly
and issued the challenge:
                              One hundred moon-white horses
to whomever will craft an ode to my kingdom!

But, he added, If the poem be poor, then so too must the poet be,
and so from him I shall seize his horse and all his property!
As the court fool reenacted the offer
the king sat down, sipping his wine

And when the chuckles died,
among the hundred guests, only one slowly rose to his feet—
Simonides of Ceos
I accept your challenge my king, said the young poet

But, Your Highness, I have no horse, and only the clothes on my back
In the crowded banquet hall, many began to laugh
Silence! bellowed the king
Who among you is half as brave as this stranger with a broken tongue?

And the banquet hall fell silent
Whoever you are, wherever you are from, let the challenge then be this!
pronounced King Sopas
Should your poem please my ears, I will grant you

not one hundred white steeds, but a thousand
and my very best vineyard
All in the banquet hall gasped
But! If you fail, the king added

I will take not your filthy sandals, nor the rope you wear as a belt
But instead, I will take your life
Brave foreigner, do you accept?
After a moment, Simonides of Ceos

closed his eyes
The great hall now like a tomb
And, hoarse at first, the poet's words
began—

Steady as the streams and rivers
of his description, soon graduating over rocks
to the mountains he'd crossed, the starry wheels
of a thousand skies; wildflowers

in symphonic fields of thriving honeycomb;
every fig cart and boat rattled aboard
for two years to arrive at this very moment
with adoration for his newfound home . . .

And when Simonides opened his eyes again,
not even the servants' shuffling could be heard
And through silent tears, the banquet guests turned
to Sopas in his throne

Well done, said the king
But for however beautiful your words, all the mountains,
birds, clouds, trees, fields, and seas . . . not *once*
in *all* my kingdom's grandeur, did you mention me

Simonides lowered his head to prepare for death
But, because you are a stranger to this land, continued the king,
I will spare your superfluous words and ignorance
Be gone with you, while you can, and never ever return . . .

And through a gauntlet of jeers, mockery, and spit,
Simonides the Wandering Poet of Ceos!
made his way out of the palace
Soon the banquet resumed

More music, wine, laughter, celebration . . .
That night, as Simonides slept at the foot of an olive tree,
there was a crash in the distance
Then another, and again

Screams as if transported on wings
Battered harps and drums—
The roof of King Sopas's great banquet hall
was collapsing!

But only just before dawn,
as the family members arrived with torches
in search of their loved ones,
did true hopelessness set in

How can we find anyone?
wailed the seekers
All the bodies are charred, crushed,
drowned in rubble!

And once again,
from shadows, Simonides of Ceos
stepped forward, eyes burning
closed, to slowly resee

not between buckled pillars
in the vicinity of the fallen crown,
or any famous general's uniquely studded sword
on its demolished dais,

but far toward a nameless servant's shy
raven braid, the gap in her
smile, a tiny wine-
colored birthmark on cold smashed cheek

the poet cleared with trembling
fingers for the polestar
back, this time
to a hundred holy

mangled
states of grace

Lottery

Wait and see

also the night's dead

stars increasing the odds

of your birth

The Book of Blackouts

We kept wading farther out
We not we, but our sloshy heaves
goosefleshing into little locks
under cool, moonlit lake

                        This country
isn't ready for us, you said,
luxurious, recidivistic; I remember
thinking your dream-yelps afterward
must be your Viet father on fire
But maybe your Hmong mother's third marriage
equally fixed you for life
Tomboy   Two nooses of black braids
all July tempting the entire Metro bar   Gone
Torched one Sunday dawn for the insurance

Every world has its devils
You won't escape these anymore
than you'll capture them

Now I see what you meant when you said
we should have another superpower
after invisibility or
absolutely nothing
                        Blacks & Indians

in this town billeted inside white guilt
We should have pain-love & longing-anger
like ice cubes in warm beer   We should
have women who don't destroy their men
as if soldiers trained by their jungle-soaked fathers
We should expect no one
will understand this; press our own
sweet confections from the inverse molds
of these stale dark emotions
no American History book will ever reference

Tonight, I'll resee
for all this snowy black highway speed
your sister's Jesus hands shaking over your stitched forehead
It's unclear where
we took different turns twelve years back
in the Book of Blackouts

But know I still replay your soul's
algorithm on the drums of my migraines
only your so kissable fingertips knew
the secret barometric combination to

Tonight I'll eat my sleep
& revise us resurfacing
from that snow ditch where they finally found
your thug-wannabe brother clawed
& shot in the leg, stomach, fist—

The tip-money drawer we promised

not to touch for three months

will not end up stolen with the microwave & VCR

Your German-Irish stepfather won't leave your mother

for a new refugee from Thailand

Your financial aid won't get cut

I won't take up cards

No one will stain anyone's boss or best friend

We'll wreck our knees at temple

And I promise

I'll finally understand

                All this sadness

did not eventually drown

our love—no,

like a knife, it contained

each sin

String Theory

As a boy, I chose a beach ball
with a metal chopstick
over food & grown-ups
What wouldn't float away
despite any mouth
Some things choose us
Waking in a best friend's coffin
Falling asleep in a too-thin language
The slow, inward draw of a lover's
draining dream
Feathery rain that will never land
Sweet dry leaf sage translucent silver-
fish flee still dispatching oceans
Each time I burn the world pure
When the Lord created the sun
shadows unfastened themselves
Let there be the mature mind
Some things won't return
Let there be the unquenchable sea
Let there be an infant somewhere, always
in the city night, refusing to obey
He will speak through scissors
He will collect infinitely useless string
He will fashion a kind of belief
in subtraction's eloquence

2

Mourning in Altaic

During the last month my father was alive, I sat up with him during the evenings, trying to conjure questions I'd for years been meaning to ask him about the Korean War. He'd never spoken a word about it. But looking at the scars scissoring up to his throat and the strain on his brow to keep the constant pain at bay, the idea now of probing, after so many years, felt invasive. I remembered all the times he'd inquired about my life; the indignant grunts I'd given in reply.

Then one evening, without warning, he spoke. It was one of those rare times—his insides at peace; enough nutrients and neurotransmitters flowing through his blood and brain to render him fully lucid.

I was trying to reread my favorite Gogol story, "The Carriage."

"Mom said you're writing a novel," he whispered, dry-mouthed, without opening his eyes—his voice almost completely gone.

"Just some poems."

He swallowed, and began slowly moving the healing stone over his chest. My sister had given the smooth gray object to him when he'd first been diagnosed with throat cancer several months earlier. At first, he'd scoffed at it, but now it seemed a natural extension of his hand.

"Try to marry a Korean girl," he added, out of nowhere.

Emboldened by this rare mood, or maybe sensing vulnerability opening between us, I asked him as gently as I could where he wanted to be buried when the time came—a question my sister and mother had refused to even think about.

He opened his eyes and considered it, as if for the first time, blinking at the ceiling.

"Maybe by water," he finally said, closing his eyes again. "I don't know."

He grimaced from a sudden flare of pain.

To change the subject, I asked what he thought about all day. The good things. Here. Now. With his eyes closed most of the time.

I suppose I was still hoping to hear something about his childhood or adolescence. Lost years that I've always thought could have served as guideposts.

"What gives you some, any kind of relief?"

After a moment, a faint smile eased the strain on his forehead.

"Hunting, fishing," he said, without opening his eyes. The stone now lay caged inside his fingers on his bony chest. "With you guys. So cute. All of us. Good things like that."

To fill the late nights while my father was dying, I watched a lot of TV, gorging on the light and sound—though the most prominent image I recall now is a bad dream he had in which a shadowy figure behind a snowblower entered his room.

"Should not have eaten," he mumbled, when I came in to see what was wrong.

He'd only had a few sips of the beef and soy sauce broth I'd made. I pulled my chair up closer beside his bed. "Why don't you try visualizing?"

On her last visit, my sister had taught him how to imagine his insides healing.

"Doesn't work."

"What about meditating?"

"Doesn't work."

I reached over and shaped his thumbs and middle fingers so they touched as two individual circles. "Hold your fingers together like this."

I began a simple chant.

I knew from my mother that his father had been an old-school Confucian, his mother a Buddhist who'd also practiced shamanic animism, and his older sister was a Christian. But he and I had never discussed these things. My mother, a Christian, had always been in charge of spiritual matters in our household.

"What's that language?" he whispered, in Korean.

"Pali."

"It sounds old."

For some reason, while trying to pass the hours during this time, I had trouble concentrating when reading. My eyes kept running off the page, no matter which book I picked up; the voices all so far away, as if I couldn't fully comprehend the English language. As if something inside me and connected to my father in the next room was dissolving.

One night I searched his bookshelves for something to read in Korean, and came upon the tattered jokbo my mother had presented me when I'd turned sixteen. Four bound volumes of my particular Lee (Yi) clan genealogy. My paternal grandmother had given them to my aunt, to give to my mother, to pass on to me when she deemed the time was right. In the jokbo, as my mother explained, my family's bloodline was recorded by birth date, hometown, education, titles, and accomplishments, if any— seven centuries back to the Koryo Dynasty.

My Korean name still appears as the final entry.

But my interest was really only piqued when my mother mentioned that my older sister didn't know of the jokbo. Although the names of wives and unmarried daughters were recorded in more recent centuries, the bloodline and tradition were continued paternally. My mother described how my grandfather naturally assumed my father's older brother would pass the jokbo on to his eldest son, but that that uncle had turned into a black sheep and drunkard, bearing only one boy out of wedlock, then died shortly after the war under mysterious circumstances. My father, the only other male—the bright, younger son—had never shown much interest in the jokbo. My mother conjectured that this was in part due to the fact that he'd grown up during the brutal Japanese occupation of Korea (1910–45). As a schoolboy, one day he'd been assigned a Japanese name and grammar book, and was warned to never again speak Korean. "They destroyed so much of our culture and tradition in one generation," my mother hissed. She went on about how the Japanese subjugated, brainwashed, and exploited every soul and natural resource they could, enslaving tens of thousands of girls and young women into sexual servitude for the Imperial Japanese Army, assassinating the Korean emperor and every possible descendant, even redirecting streams and moving hills to disturb the land's natural flow of auspicious energy. "Everything twisted, screwed up," she said. "Then just when the Japanese were finally gone, now you had the Soviets and Americans dropping bombs over what they wanted to control!"

At the time, it all made little sense to me, living in Fargo, North Dakota: the jokbo's strange vertical rows of black calligraphy; the damp, rooty, medicinal scent of the thin, yellowed pages (printed and bound in the Korean year 4,291)—compiled from the many more master documents in some distant hall of records in Chungcheong Province. My mother traced her finger over the brushstrokes of a poet-ancestor, Yi Saek, from 1366 AD, and brokenly began to recite it. But I couldn't understand the poem, or any other part of the jokbo. I could barely read English. None of my friends read books. North Fargo was heavily working class. To be caught holding a book meant ridicule. From age thirteen on, we made a ritual of getting penetratingly stoned before and after school. When I look back, most who lingered loosely together were lost: stunted types of single parents, Edgewood trailer kids, mixed-race stoics, military brats, Bible refugees, drinker replicas, druggies, vandals, thieves. Nights, we'd coax anyone we could find into buying us a case of Black Label or a bottle of Everclear. We'd go down by the Red River and play punching games, belching back at a keg, or catch rides to sputter around sand dunes at the city limits. Or hang with over-blushed girls, whose smiles were slow; who alternated each other's clothes and V. C. Andrews and some novel about a woman repeatedly raping her dog. We'd dizzy hormones in moldy basements, scaling out ditchweed and crushing out lines of sleeping pills to Zeppelin, Marley, N.W.A. No one wanted to be who or where or what they were. By my freshman year, I'd been placed on criminal probation twice. One night in my junior year while my father, finally pushed to the limit, had me pinned against the basement wall with the same loaded 12-gauge he'd taught me to shoot clay pigeons with, screaming in Korean that a pending third offense would mean juvenile prison, I unleashed a drunken, slurry torrent of four-letter words back in English that stunned him long enough for me to stumble out to my rust-eaten Mercury. We lived together for another year under the same roof, until I was seventeen. But neither of us ever really came back from that night.

Maybe everyone's veins are endued with a certain historical color of light.

3

Transmelodic War Dance

It isn't fate's by-now rusty blade,
or thoughts rethought until parasites

slinging dice. But the way
we fork our peas of death

before a static-enshrouded anchorman.
What else to result from a protest

art show in the living room of a paraplegic
in green silk and egret bolo? I am here

to learn something I've been preparing to run
from my whole life. Some tally

I've regarded as someone else's broken mirror.
In a system whose white-hot core

generates ice. And here you are
renegade nurse to all the galaxy's

cadavers; eyes asizzle, breathing
anisette into my brine. Friend,

Lover, Daemon in the sense of terrible
inspiration. Here on the Lower East Side,

once the most densely populated
tract on the planet, now tight

slacks, eyelashes blessed, the last Gypsy
fortune teller an upscale burrito shack.

Cooling on Suffolk in a flat groaning
with submarine pipes, flitting

in and out of day one-hundred-four of the war marinating on TV—
I intuit: *More*

as molten you in brassiere
ponytail your hair and predict three

generations *minimum* to heal the psychic wounds.
Here where you impersonate a fire

to transmelodica as the year turns blue.
How will I ever stop you? Why

would I want to?

Neon Pyramid

The real war will never get in books. —WALT WHITMAN

Once upon a time, I bagged cowboys with a tomahawk

Now in this cold casino on a rez past midnight

                                      I too am shot
by smug expressions of Native pit bosses
at every player ready to leap chipless off a cliff

After all, why expect any sympathy for a Korean,
Black, Mexican, Somali, Lebanese—clung detritus
in the flood of passing faces on their secret video screens—who, granted,
never foraged in with beads, bullets, smallpox, & dummy contracts,
but nevertheless:

Slam dust off green felt
Curse their dealers
Snort speed in the bathrooms
Mis-cardcount with rusty brains
Always celebrating too quickly

Hard to blame them

No one expects a body's organs to float you this far
into prairie hinterland from Midwestern
common sense

But tonight the heart
is a drunken, belligerent bus driver—
Cordoned off
in High Stakes mid-July, stranded
by wars & lost marriages, layoffs, cost of power
& gas, businesses
belly-up, or just retired low-
fat boredom & a life played equally bad
Sometimes they speak,
a player's shadow language: massaging
past lives furrowed in brows—

I Iran & hate both a Arab & the Jew

Luck is a river's fishes

Hey, my cleavage is the happy cadaver of a famous bank robber!

Tolstoy, you ragged, onion-reeking Cossack, what
would you minister to these fellow congregants
in this last resort antichurch? I've seen you

dragging your oxygen tank to & from the Wild Sevens slot island
three nights in a row before they stretchered you out
unconscious in the same clothes
Is God really dead,
or the killer capitalistic streak, this flashing jackpot, that behemoth
bingo payout turning wrists & retinas to stone?

Fortunately, tonight it doesn't matter, because

Dostoevsky, broken addict extraordinaire, is here

third shift, Windexing mirrored pillars, scanning

the carpet for butts & a stray

chip every several years

                        Little Father, what wisdom

have you for me tonight other than to drink

my bitter milk & stand up straight

or else?

         All I wanted was ease

from boiling dreams, & now

the self-same thirty-two pop song loop

has satellite-beamed into our wheezing;

the entire kingdom at a toxic symbiosis—

                                Desperation recirculating cool desire

The Buddhist to my right bets table max then stands,

all four feet six—a sugar beet farmer who'd eat your car

to survive; whose circular, chain-smoking stories resemble

a Shanghai river at dawn

Or take the cowgirl cursing in Spanish to my left, surely a heart

of amber with that eyeliner, accompanied by rotating

twenty-something white men to bear witness & light her menthols—big sister

to regret, busty grandmother to shame, in black knee-high boots, maybe once a prostitute, but now just a solid third-base tablemate;

greedy, but at least consistent in her hits & stays,

attuned to the rhythm of our four-deck like a drum machine

Tonight, no open seat for loneliness

As long as you play,

announces this Cleopatra cardslinger with the prettiest flow of turquoise nails

Did we just trade retorts & hand signals as if bathing spirits

two hours & only once did our knuckles

kiss?

       Or were we laughing at each other's angels?

Because I am dying

             to know what will become of all this hope

Can the heart decay waiting?

Or like the somber Crip with a queen diamond

& six spade tattooed on his neck, his plaintive chant:

every minute is a worse-possible hand—

                    Will it too slink

away its aging display of faded images?

Or sit here forever

        sipping bright-green anger?

Past 4 a.m., every face a refugee of human features

                                            And I know:

you can't win the past

               or stalk redemption

But neither does death get any cheaper

Like the young mechanic
who hit the Super Bond 007 jackpot,
but wasn't of legal age to collect—

                        Come back

the next night, a sawed-off shotgun
stroking his thigh

                  Or so everyone loves to tell

The point: anyone could win big at any time!
Most will crawl back into their shells
& sputter home

                 Others will die

dreaming of free liquor & smoke
Mortgages, partnerships, retirements—in a cloud

Some, like this fake-baked pregnant girl
even joke-threaten she'll call the FBI
for fraud

           as she hits

                  & her mascara soon melts

But none at this hour will hand over fear

                                    without a fight

All I have

               is my life

Karaoke Poem

Tonight I will find the one
karaoke song, the sole melody to summarize the rest of my life.
Romantic is fine; tinny okay too. Soul. Rock. Hip-hop. Even country.
I'm open as a kimchi taco truck lost in Arkansas. Graceful
how lightning dominatrixes thunder. Tears of rain. Ever notice
a person sings the way they make love? Zeus on the ceiling
of the Sistine Chapel had game. I don't like a show.
I like slow, buttery vowels. But do jackpot your eyes
starward. The French call orgasm *the little death*.
After I die, I'd like to master ventriloquism. I'd like to hear
someone named Chavandarinsulanix discover
a new planet in some relevant solar system. Or common
terminal disease. Tonight I will sing like no one has ever sung.
Or a song no one would ever sing. Same thing. Like being in love
with the wrong person. She was in love with disgrace.
From the x-ray, she chose my heart & punctured lung.
We kissed while a sea of warm poplars ascended stairs
to the moon. Argued how to paint a wound.
We went bowling & drank. (We think we know
how to let go on time, but everything comes back:
balls, pins, victims like fans screaming on a roadside.) Eventually,
she remembered her zip code. I retain a French
horn, blood orange, & locket of synapses. Smart
people don't seek out others' emotions on stage.

Like a daily salad over chocolate-&-beef sautéed arteries.
In Korean slang, if you sleep with a person, you "eat" them.
In English, it involves turning a tool. I've never understood
musicians who can't notate or play an instrument. Apparently,
karaoke can make a star or meal or home improvement
project of anyone. Good preachers
pablumize others' secrets & sins. Artists
of divine refreshment. Prisoners of what Shakespeare would call essential
play. He dressed young boys as women & filled them
with poetry. Maybe there is no one song
for anyone. My song. Our song. I'm troubled
by couples, neither of whom will sing "their" song aloud.
But I love it when a woman sings a man's song. Or vice
versa. A thing of equilibrium clicks inside both ears,
& momentarily it's crystal clear. Like when
the lights come on at 1:52 a.m. We are all just
new shadows, dressed in ancient songs.
Shadows that contain in our pockets
hard love to hold the heart
up when gone.

When the Lights Rereveal the City

I was falling   I didn't know from where   to when

Heart eating throat   body plummeting   I might have flapped my arms

but was ashamed

                        I've heard of flight attendants who die saving passengers' lives

As soon as the screaming child or fat man gets rebuckled in the aircraft

hits a jet stream   plunges   the flight

attendant falls

            upward

                     at 870 m.p.h. & dies like a geyser of flesh & untrained regrets

People fall all the time

                Civilizations

                         Sumeria, Rome, Karakorum, Portugal

Historians' reputations   A nation's   ability to smile   for no reason

Once I saw a bag lady seated on cracked concrete in the middle of a public zoo

Splayed marionette legs   She wore Prada, couture, & one torn nylon

The other naked shin   banana-blue-black   A gray wig burdened her head

A lovely spirit I thought surrounded by the suffocation of moldy fur

I wanted to give a dollar   yet not offend   Some people

       fall their whole lives & don't even know it   Used

car & mortgage salesmen   like my cousin & his friends   Smiling

                                   as they fall away

one word & vice-grip at a time   Alcoholics   Crack

H   unlike some believe   is not used to feel good   but break

the falling that feels too helpless   A psychic & spiritual net

of molecules   symphonized in space   A friend once said

God is like gravity   Obey & float   Try to fly

& be emptied   impaled   scraped away from your own image

We were standing on that sake brewery's rooftop in Berkeley   I replied God

was the wind   Each time I took a walk   Divine urging in my face

on my flanks   If only you could align that with your goals   She said

you're full of it   We drank our warm beers & watched the stars fall

And ten months later she was carbon across miles or years of the Pacific's floor

                                        A slow

sedimentary fall   Of all spikes   a needle is only one

But maybe even a tornado   couldn't have broken her fall through those dark

mothy months   If I'm honest   my words

at the end when she'd vomit all my granola & beer   were tacks & nails

Sometimes when alone I wonder what I'd reach for if the earth opened wide

A friend's husband died down a sinkhole ticking under their linoleum

                                   I try to note

all I have   Books   A well-used aloe plant   Artifacts & scents & mental images of bodies   to catch   before the dark dirt   sifts into my pores

Physicists say the world & everything in it is   falling through space   No

one says hearts molt wings at different rates   No one talks of shame

improving a singer's grace   No one says time is the only god

writing regularly   back   No one tells you your mind

is the wind falling & rising   Subsiding   Due to passengers

Silences in a story too dense   A half-decade   maybe burnt solid   But

eventually some force   seems to   Love,

     I am airborne   I am wings & no one's heart

I am heat & this winter afternoon

     I don't know who you are anymore

Man on Steppe

Somewhere a DJ is thinking
too much, you can hear, working
shit out, tormenting
the final sweaty bodies like a cold
ripe wheat field. Vova, Yelena, and I
smoke, stumble this bitter-
frost junkyard. It's dawn
and I could drown in your fire-blue
arteries. A fuselage, or hang-
man of rust, reminds
in 500 years the world will survive
only if I sheet-metal my heart
into the delicate shape
of your anvil. Maybe
the Communists failed. And yet
these burnt-out stadiums like eyes
once sparked all night
with ten thousand coarse, party-
woven suits, dresses, and uniforms
for apparatchik poets dramatizing
the future of grain. Likewise
the DJ knows he's a waning god
chiming East European techno
like a dozen dead chain gangs on crank.

If I close my eyes, I can step into a future
when "Soviet" conjures "American."
"Chinese" equals "Mexican." "Germany"
and "Paraguay" speak as one. Here,
on Tundra Mars, where all morning
ashen economists and physicists
plant new ideas behind the sun,
and the moon is a harpsichord on fire,
revised by trees so green they're blue;
by night each fermented body
an amp plugged into the neighboring nuclear
plant. Crackling inside,
when they sing, they turn
off all apartment lights
and let their lungs slowly
glow. And their little children
do not live in bodies, but
institutions overgrown at the edges
with hair and bone and vandalized
murals. And far away, cloaked in smoke,
a Tatar warrior steadies his mare, lights
a joint, and ponders
all the little sails racing
to and from the eyes of strangers.

Sand Camouflage Elegy

Never mistake uncertainty for dawn
or dusk as your life in reverse

The soul, sand-whipped by noon, hides
from the self's sharper shadows

Unsuppered as any hot ghost in a bombed-out window

Step through night, stunned, yes
now

while your marrow is still sweet
from an earth's smoldering core

Time—a trick of breath and light
stretching retinas like a mask

Meanwhile, cools a great invisible castle
with tragic stories for its invisible bricks

Fused by tears, bile, pus, and shit—

Last week at the funeral, we all sucked
in and out a vaguely differentiated chant

His name fragrant, incense
ember fishing over sightless skin
and sweaty rice cakes

Or religion maybe this: we all slide
back down our shadows of birth
in the enemy's uniform

And it matters only
on eternity's hot wave
you kissed the grenade back

and never why
or where

Buddhist, Christian, Muslim, etc.—
In whatever sector
of the soul tonight
you relight the body's need
to glow

At "Last Boshintang Restaurant" in Seoul

Sipping dog stew is a little
like watching soldiers kill
& die on the nightly news

Stringy mouthfuls somewhere
between steer, snake, greasy
politician, & sweet pet
pig

Maybe you'd rather not
have another serving,
but eventually you
can get used to it

Four Orders of Silence

The exterminator arrived
to seal the crevices under our eaves
with stocking-like fishnets

They fly out, he assured, and can't
come back

For days I listened to infant bats
trapped in the walls
                            Their mammalian
mothers attacking a corner
streetlamp with claws and
tiny teeth

By winter, only snow
on black mountains

A coal train
scraping past

Spice in my dead father's
blue sweater the last

time he visited
and asked me to oil
a hinge in my heart

Regenesis

At the Kumgang pharmacy
on Broadway, my love smiles, and so I do
purchase the tiny aluminum spoon
that could feed crumbs to an ant.

Not quite the sterling silver tool
my mother would lift from among her rings,
summoning me twice as often
in summertime.

Nor is mine the fragrant hush of her lap,
padded with the small pillow
of a twice-birthed gut.

In truth, only this seriousness
in wielding a deadly means
with such exacting sweeps
remains—
                    sweet cat-
licks inside the ear, that
ethereal kissing
you say feels like making love to the wind.

Once upon a time, I
pacify, surgically scraping,
a seed formed in God's ear.

As once my mother intoned.

The seed fell to the soil and the first animal was born.

What kind of animal?
you ask, unable
to see me.

A bear. No, a tiger—

Male or female?

Just hold still.

What is love if all the details retreat
down a hole?
                    Furtive
moments when the heart, daily hunted,
waits like a bird,
                    watching, watching?

Where did that boy who twice ran away
to live inside grocery displays
go?

And the woman who bore him,
did she promise or threaten
to leave him there forever
alone?

But, alas, I come up
empty—palming
no sweet or rough
kernel from the ripeness of this body
I am learning to love as deep
as perhaps only a mother
should dare to reach.

I don't know.

No matter.
Smiling, eyes
still closed,
         you roll
as if to offer another
pot of gold.

Dream After Watching Nine Ozu Films
One Weekend & Considering Imperial Japan's
Response to the West's Colonization of 85% of
the Pre-WWII World (Alone Over Beer & Falafel)

"Idealism & nostalgia, two opposing eyes."

Yellow canaries grow neurons by learning new songs.
Beauty kills old ones in smoky karaoke bars.

"I'm dying in reverse, often it seems."

Then it rained on the beer commercial models in double time.

"One rarely hears silence's worm."

Nineteen thousand two-hundred seventy-one cherry blossoms
waving good-day!

Things that continue postmortem:
fingernails, gossamer hair, the rare bone
cell, an urge
to view the world at waist level.

"Abundances of arboreal & nocturnal flying insects
differ little between the forest edge & interior." (trans.)

"Like Crohn's Disease?"

No, as an imaginary planet of black-&-white, skin-musk ghosts.

More than one's will, what tends to work
are a few simple grooming gestures.

Quietly kaleidoscopic; an oil lamp–lit lotus pond
in late spring dense with fireflies & plankton . . .

Setsuko returns home from the picnic to find
the camera has eaten her father & is panning
back toward her body folding into a field
of chrysanthemums.

"All left behind for someone else's great-grandson
    to breathe upon a dragonfly's wing."

Epilogue:

"No, it was only after the second war that sound meant something again."
The long empty highway, clouds incandescent, telephone poles
forlorn like every home's half-built fence.

Cut to: Drunken kabuki actor
on a bicycle, whistling
a tune no one wishes to remember the true melody to . . .

"The Shochiku Film Company? Yes,
most regrettable for any monumental Tokyo office to receive
reconstruction in a Godzilla set."

GI Joseph B—, the Taliban, & Poontang

U.S. military presence in South Korea: 1945–present

The room was a closet with theater-
like props—table lamp, water basin, bleached

towels, bed, & alarm clock
so you don't buck long. Reminds me

of eighth grade when I got cast
as Cassio in Des Plaines, IL— Tack-

titted Biancas leaping on your back as you pass
their pink-neon window fronts

lining the bordello warrens.
At first these thonged, stuck-up model types

wouldn't touch us servicemen from the States. Left us
to the pockmarked pincushions

cockroaching the base. Then
the economic bubble burst.

Suddenly they know your rank.
But beware, these bitches will slip

a collar on you all the way back.
Lifetimes feistier than any Manila girl

stained in Catholic lace. Before
complacent, Koreans get anxious—a good

emotion to work with. The world
is too afraid. North Korea?

No Great Dictator, no reason
for us to jack off here.

Then China moves in.
Containment. You see?

We feed the fat fucker his nuclear-
dipped Swedish blondes

& starve all possible opposition.
You see, History is a thing

you knead like clay or bread
in bare hands, tenderly,

until broken down
to a pliable desire.

Those grunts in Iraq
who stuck that steamy

mutton twat
then offed her parents,

what did anyone expect?
Hidden scissors or IED

ice to melt your face in a flash.
In a land where women

are wrapped like useless
Christmas presents. The mind

is a heat-seeking organ.
But here's the real secret

in war, politics, life:
all weakness eventually wants

to get caught, annihilated,
or exploited.

In two years I'll rank
sergeant. My fiancée

back home believes it
could be one if I pray.

Sometimes I see her face
floating through Uijeongbu markets

in a sea of black heads.
So white,

almost blue.

If in America

Hmong Hunter Charged With 6 Murders
Is Said to Be a Shaman —NEW YORK TIMES

If a tree falls in a forest,
does it make a sound?

If a rifle fires a shot in the woods,
whose body first hits the ground?

If a group of angry hunters
surrounds, curses at, and accosts you
for wandering onto their land

If you apologize for being lost,
inform you saw no posted signs, swallow
their chinks this and gooks taking over that;
are walking away over mud and fallen leaves when a loud
crack far behind you kicks up black earth

If your father was conscripted to fight
on the side of the United States
for the CIA during the war in Vietnam

If he, your mother, you—the oldest son—
and all your younger siblings were later abandoned
in the hills of Laos as targets for genocide by the Viet Cong

If after five years in a Thai refugee camp,
you come to this land as a teen, a casualty
of history and time, then receive three years
of training to become a sharpshooter
in the u.s. military

If you spent your adolescence watching blacks,
Asians, Latinos, and whites watching one
another watch each other for weakness and flaws

If, after this first blast, you wheel
around in a bright orange vest; glimpse
in that split second an angry, possibly
inebriated man lowering *or* resighting his rifle

If, in that icy moment, you recall
the Native friend you used to collect cans with;
once watched his three-hundred-pound father
unload himself from a Chevy Impala and chase
the boy down University with a ball-peen hammer

If, of your own children, your quietest
son lately lacks the wherewithal at school
to defend himself; and your oldest daughter
has always been for some inexplicable reason
ashamed of you

If hunting for you is not just a sport;
never a time to drink beers
with friends in a cabin, but rather
is a factor in considering your family's winter protein consumption

If you believe in God, but not the good in everyone

If you hate to think about this shit, because
why the fuck is it always on you
to preprove your loyalty and innocence?

If—frightened for your life and
the livelihood of your immediate and extended
family—in that split second, you reel
and train your own gun back at the far face
of that vapory barrel now aiming at your own

If, yes, you are sometimes angry and so look forward
to escaping your truck driver's life on certain
designated dates, on certain designated
lands, not always clearly demarcated, but always clearly stolen
from the ancestors of fat drunk red men
so confused they chase their own firey songs
in the form of their sons

Stolen from generations of skewed black backs,
hunched your whole life on street corners laughing
and picking their bones

Stolen from the paychecks of your brown coworker
social security ghosts

Stolen like your own people
from mountains in one land
only to be resettled and resented here
in projects and tenements

If you barely finished high school, but you know
from all you've ever seen of this system
Might Makes Right,
and excuses, treaties, and cover-ups
appear the only true code inscribed on most white men's souls

If, after such slurs, pushes, and threats in these woods
it is now also on you to assess
if that far rifle still locked on your face
just issued a mistake, a warning
shot, or murderous attempt—

                                        and the answer is:
your military muscle fibers
act

If you then spot three four five six seven? other
hunters now scattering for their ATVs
and, of course—if a gook,
don't be a dumb one—
scattering now also for their weapons

If you are alone in this land,
on foot, in miles of coming snow, wind, and branches
and don't even know
in which direction you'd run

If from birth you've seen
what men with guns, knives,
and bombs are capable of doing
for reasons you never wanted to understand

If in this very same county's court of all-white
witnesses, counsel, judge, and jurors
it will forever be your word against theirs
because there was no forensic testimony
over who shot first

If, yes, sometimes you can hear voices,
not because you're insane, but
in your culture
you are a shaman, a spiritual healer,
though in this very different land
of goods and fears, your only true worth
seems to be as a delivery man and soldier

If, upon that first fateful exchange in these woods,
your instinct, pushing pin to
balloon, were to tell you it's now
either you and your fatherless family of fourteen,
or *all* of them

Would *you* set your rifle down;
hope the right, the decent,
the fair thing on this buried American soil
will happen?

Or would you stay low,
one knee cold, and do
precisely as your whole life
and history have trained?

And if you did,
would anyone even care
what really happened

that afternoon
eight bodies plummeted
to earth like deer?

4

Chosun 5.0

How to ever imagine war could bloom into this

Have I eaten the wrong kind of mushroom cloud again?

The shrapnel I inherited
from my father's brain—glistening
like a microchip of the night cityscape of Seoul & her suburbs
from a helicopter the youngest sibling of my mother
owns, piloted by a former mixed martial artist in white gloves

Ironic that this uncle plays golf & chess better than his four u.s. &
Australian immigrant brother & sisters can mime their jealousy &/or
regret, in either language's subtext

War, the ultimate economic, geopolitical, slash-&-burn technique

But let's slow it down, examine these patented seeds

Rewind, back to the image of the hottie tattoo artist/DJ in Hongdae—I
ask her tarantular eyelashes what the hanja ideograms on her neck say:

"Picky viruses are waiting for an angel better than you"

Ironic that this damn story I'm writing about clones gets weaker with
each revision

Cut me open, let me see deeper into the wiring of this poem

Past the alleles—I'm talking electrons gossiping on sodium pentothal with their back panels wide open

Atomic corpses buried in tracts of broadband rental plots in the sky

Because I'm convinced something untoward is happening in that nature camp my little cousin got himself interventioned into 67 kilometers from any internet connection

I suspect it's worse than a Korean Jehovah's Witness video text, knocking on your cell's screen

Worse than plastic surgery to smooth creases on the brain

Worse than the suicide rate, one of the lowest in the 80s, now the highest in the industrialized world

Worse than K-pop rap with no concept of street cred

Worse than the very aliens this little cousin is so adept at detonating across the ecosphere

My theory: Samsung has kidnapped & is cloning then trans-racially adopting out copies of the boy to sell more video games internationally!

Tonight, I'll wander the streets of Kangnam, drunk, wondering which hallyu hairdo & butt implant best epitomizes post-post capitalism, sha-boom sha-boom!

I'll meet friends at 3:37 a.m. in Shinchon for room karaoke, later lock-stepping in a long line of other dragon-breathing castaways to be seated outdoors for spicy potato stew, serenaded by early weekday traffic, & wonder what Stalin's double whispered into Ho Chi Minh's double's ear

Capitalism at once the ringtone that flattens our dreams, & yet the only faint birdsong outside cotton fields, gulags, gas chambers, & factories of child-bone old century realism

I know even less where this ink-&-cloud dance will finally blight out some tract of honeybee parlance

But these wild, beautiful, cream-white Jindo dogs infected with worms at
    Mihwangsa temple seem to know
At night, I eat from their paws & they sing me to sleep with pine needle tea
    & the clean burn of a four-day fast
Material world
Immaterial world
Throbbing like a memory of migration's longing

Or has, once again, my faith ripped at the seams?

(Never mind my drawstring pants bigger than the largest Christian church in the world—26,000 live each Sunday morning in Yoido; 700,000 via closed circuit in all)

What is culture or history anymore, in an age when every year brings that which is twice as fast & ten times as cheap?

Meaning God's battery pack satelliting the universe may not have an unlimited warranty after all

Now I've got it: the ending to my story about clones:

One foggy night, the hero subways to Apgujeong to have dinner with his one beautiful cousin, whose father is the 32nd richest man in South Korea, along with his other beautiful cousin who grew up fatherless in a shantytown. They eat kalbi & drink yangju & sing & argue over social politics, multinational corporate conspiracies, God's gold standard, Buddhist oligarchies, & at one point during the night, homeboy glances at these two young women's illogically similar eyelids & noses, shakes his blurry head, & realizes the only way to become fully incarnate is to jam a scalpel in the very biotechnological dynamo in the sky that automatically updates the mind's yearly operating system

Memory a leaky, zinc-green wound

Far from Xanadu

What are we waiting for, assembled in the forum?
The barbarians are due here today . . .

. . .

And now, what will happen to us without barbarians?
They were, those people, a kind of solution.
—C. P. CAVAFY, "Waiting for the Barbarians"

What are we waiting for atop this final ridge?

The Great Khan is still convening with his generals and advisors;
his religious men and all his sons in the royal tent.

What could they possibly have to discuss so long? Behold the majesty of
our army, as far as the eye can see. Every soldier's face wrought with pride
and glory.

Perhaps new dangers to consider in this kingdom. And do not
confuse pride with lust. I speak of those whose taste for silver is
stronger than glory or blood.

They are young. As we were when our village first was burned. There, who
is that regal figure in the golden chair at the city's main gate below?

By the bauble on his head, the many scrolls in his lap, he must be
their famed emperor, maybe their pope.

Fools, how can paper and crosses bind any right to land and sky?

Perhaps the Great Khan is still angered by the last village we burned. Everything, even the young men with their weapons laid down; the fresh maidens; all the fields of grain and livestock.

Their rebel leaders should have agreed to our terms. We are glorious. Look at our uniforms, once coarse leather, now excellent chain and onyx. Who can stop us from conquering this city and the next, until the earth is one empire united!

Or perhaps His Greatness's concerns have nothing to do with these people below. Regard well the very faces among us, all around. Can you not hear the low cacophony of variously muttering tongues?

From whatever city and nation, all have sworn their allegiance. Like our own, their loyalty is golden.

Ah, loyalty not to whom, but to what?

Xanadu, and the greatest empire mankind has ever known! Fool, where is your mind?

Perhaps it is nothing. Perhaps our leader is only discussing the best strategy with his generals, as in days of old.

Look, now, there—
But why have the princes unfastened their chainmail? Not a single quiver slung on our generals' backs! Even the haughty advisors walk mute, ashen, with heads lowered like dogs.

Now the Great Khan himself. All bow!!!

When has our leader become so withered and grave, stroking such a long white beard?

Shhh. Now he approaches the platform.

We are poised. The enemy weeps with fear. If we fail to advance, mark my words, they will soon attack our outposts.

Dangerous, these murmurs, and growing.

Why does he not silence them? Why does he just stand there, unadorned, like a common beggar, gazing at the sky?

Perhaps our leader has finally become the god he was always said to be.

God or madman, what will become of us if he is lost? If there is no land to conquer, no new kingdoms?

A new empire will of course arise. Until then, perhaps there is work down in this city below.

Man, where is your pride, your loyalty? Are we not the most feared conquerors the world has ever known!

The only other option is perhaps to journey home.
Though, truth be told, I never really trusted or cared for those people.

Learning to Love
—for JMS

Once I loved the way my father had been pickpocketed in an enormous, bustling, anonymous city, because it meant we had nothing but one another to see us through a night long and strange, filled with new, unforeseeable love and kindness.

*

Occasionally on the subway at rush hour I want to break the strap and just hold loosely my purse. Then I remember to count and recount the exact contents of my heart, over and over, until the urge subsides and I am home and love my life again.

*

I'm happy. This method is unfailingly, always just barely enough.

Burnt Offering: Mid-November

All these Great Plains towns midday
on Main Street like faded breaths
full of frost, alcohol, & train wrecks.
An old lady pulls up in a 20-year-old mint-condition Cadillac.
This guzzling vessel she shores at the Eagle Eye Diner—
hungry ancestor of another
engine spewing black
flies over bison blinking in grass
a century & a half ago—Could she
& her kin ever dance beside any
non-white dream?

                    Howsitgoing? I say.
The old woman's vermilion frown cuts me,
then looks away. She, the bad
lover never tickled face-to-face
with a world so sweetly in flames—
Candy-white Swedish mother of grain, in a sky-
blue tractor of history. Her pork-bellied farmer
husband hobbling over a cane eyes me
as they enter for coffee & raisin cream pie.
Got a buck man? I say,
but they're already inside
the warm oven of their lives—

                              In the street
I light a torn cigarette
& rise
to new heights.

Oedipus in the Former Soviet Kazakhstan

The theater was old, soul-soiled, players
having worked their lines into the pre-Revolution wood, reliving
death until that too for them was true. We all practice
regret, but some art maybe reconstitutes it. Sky
in that part of Almaty always the color of sink water
after shaving. You'd watch them shunting in the side door
as if hunted sheep. Only a few had gravely mutable spirits—
Sergei, Kairat, Marina—gravitas like an aching canon.
But I wanted to be the crooked Erbol with heart
soaked in gasoline. Every cigarette & gesture
a borrowed Red Army of spirits. So in tune
he'd forget to groom his Muslim shepherd's self in the kiosk bar
when you went to shake his feminine hand afterward. Once
he confided he gave away some possession before every play's
opening night. Superstition. A watch, the bottle, a favorite Pioneer pin. I pointed
at the vodka in his hand. *Ahh, it creeps back*
during those off, lackluster performances; eventually,
you're married with child, turning knobs at the local plant, blind.
I laughed, thinking he'd reanimated a human grouse.
All gone now, for a Szechuan fish & chips chain. I love fish,
but if I walked inside I suspect my meal
would cry. For all those Sunday matinees I prayed
to be devastated, ripped open
by men & women with harm & defeat

in cut-glass eyes. Look at me,
I am Ideologies & Empires
collapsing, streaming
through twill, silk, sweat, spit, & this,
I knew, I too would always worship:
such a beautiful & flimsy moon.

Ode to Bruce Lee

Thank you Bruce Lee for fucking
    up my childhood like a cinderblock.
For all the whaaahs & hi-yahs. Of course,
    you choked on the mask they handed you as the Green

Hornet's sidekick Kato like some retro-
    demoted role for Tonto. So you pitched the TV
show *Kung Fu*, though in the end they cast
    David Carradine instead of you. Thank you

for hightailing it back to Hong Kong, jaw of revenge;
    where not even Kareem's sky-long footprint
could walk on you. Born in San Francisco, buried in
    Seattle, raised a Chinese nationalist in Kowloon. Thank you

for Jeet Kune Do. For teaching Chuck Norris
    how to star in abdominal reduction commercials.
For your Cantonese opera star father and Asian American
    mother. Flunked-out, Catholic-school street brawler.

Thank you for being accepted by blacks
    before whites. For quadruple-clawing the face
of the world. For training every red-blooded (Asian)
    American boy the (shadowy) sidle of a (double-edged) warrior. For knowing

who you were when everyone else was just too damn slow. Adulterer
     to your American wife; race traitor to your Taiwanese lover. Flesh
Sculpture of Blurry Art. Contradiction. Enigma. Flawed
     Heart of Sandalwood. Thank you

for hiding your quarter-German ancestry to learn Wing Chun. Fighting
     later to train Caucasians, but only certifying as instructors
Asians. Assassin. Asshole. Hero. A thousand
     stereotypes smashed over the cranium. Thank you

for not being Jackie Chan. Instead sexy, short, & slight,
     yet cut as a Ginsu knife. For never taking your eye off the Man
as you bow, always attempting to edify before you have to kill him.
     Monk. Health fanatic. Pot smoker. Sometimes my father

snuck soda & beer to go with our popcorn. Past midnight,
     we'd amble out, the only two extras to survive a forgotten war and
Monday's playground. Thank you for broken English & a hustler's flow, sung
     with limbs & a scream beyond any color or gender barrier. Charlatan

whenever they had the real you cornered. Boxing
     & cha cha champion. Style of no style. Teacher, waiter,
perennial student, philosopher. Dragon,
     you lone mirror shard in a 70s u.s. balloon-obsessed crowd. Snapping

labyrinth of gestures—ironic, iconic, loud. Flinch
     each time some dumbass kid asked me if I was related to you.
But most of all, Bruce, thank you
     for advancing on to that final island mist in the sky

& taking as many of us as you could with you.

Post Race

rainbow

elbow grease

naked

sort value: [$]_____

whose cunning?

Emergency Care

Slumped inside Hennepin County Emergency,
my eyes wander the glassy others, unmoored,
each with no self to call whole at 3 a.m.—
Salvation shudders

blanketing hope to the bomb-riffs of CNN
Sore Face, Wild Eagle-Eyed, Prosthetic Foot, and Shinplate Airing Itself
A black woman dripping red cornrows convenes
unconsciously with Jesus's mangled amber mullet

The room, a marrow broth mid-December,
sweet, decades beyond lust
Or is this soulless cinderblock building
the warm, artful heart of God

billowing a dozen white curtains?
The grand prize: a mind hot
and cold as jubilant sirens
deliver a third body's bullets

Meanwhile, the moon
recycles old love through metallic ventricles;
casts shadows around shrunken
kidneys and livers alcoholic

An infant, bundled in the self-inked, AIDS-gaunt arms
of a Native woman, mewls
a dilapidated tune; reaches up
at a soft-snoring Somali girl's sky-blue headscarf—

The doctor gives me more pills
when I tell him sometimes I see ghosts

Poetry Is a Sickness

You write not what you want,
but what flaws flower from rust

You want to write about the universe,
how the stars are really tiny palpitating ancestor hearts
watching over us

and instead what you get on the page
is that car crash on Fourth and Broadway—
the wails of the girlfriend or widow,
her long lamentation so sensuous
in terrible harmony with sirens in the distance

Poetry is a sickness

You want to write about Adoration,
the glistening sweat on your honey's chest
in which you've tasted the sun's caress,
and instead what you get
is a poem about the first of four times
your mother and father split up

Want to write about the perfection of God
and end up with just another story
of a uniquely lonely childhood

If I had a dime for every happy poem I wrote
I'd be dead

Want to write about the war, oppression, injustice,
and look here, see, what got left behind
when all the sand and dust cleared
is the puke-green carpet in the Harbor Lights Salvation Army treatment center
A skinny Native girl no older than seventeen
braids the reddish hair
of her little four- or five-year-old Down's Syndrome daughter

Outside, no blinking stars
No holy kiss's approach
Only a vague antiseptic odor and Christian crest on the wall staring back at you

I didn't say all this to that dude who sent me his poems
from prison

You want everyone to feel empowered
Want them to believe there is beauty locked in amber
inside each of us, and you chip away at that shit
one word at a time
You stampede with verbs, nouns, and scalpel adjectives
Middle-finger your literalist boss
Blow grocery cash on library fines
Sprain your left knee loading pallets all day for Labor Ready
You live in an attic for nine years
You go bankrupt
You smoke too much

Drink too much
Alienate family and friends
Say yes, poetry is a sickness, but fuck it
Do it long enough, and I promise like an anti-superhero
your secret power will become loss

Loss like only old people must know
when the last red maple on the block goes

and the drizzle turns to snow

Maybe the best poem is always the one you shouldn't have written

The ghazal that bled your index finger
Or caused your sister to reject your calls for a year
The sonnet that made the woman you loved fear
That slam poem you're still paying for
The triolet that smiled to violate you
through both ears

But Poet, Sucker, Fool
It's your job
to find meaning in all this because
you are delusional enough to believe
that, yes, poetry is a sickness,
but somehow if you can just scrape together enough beauty and truth

to recall, yes, that Broadway car crash was fucked up,
but the way the rain fell to wash away the blood
not ten minutes after the ambulance left
was gorgeous

Or how maybe your mother and father would sometimes scream,
but also wrapped never-before-seen tropical
fruit for one another every Xmas Eve

How in the morning before opting out I watched
that tiny Native girl fumbling
to braid her own and her now-
snoring mother's long black hair
together
          in a single cornrow—

If I can just always squiggle
down like this:
                even half as much
as what I'd otherwise need
to forget

maybe these scales
really will one day tip
to find each flaw that made us

Exquisite

Noir

The sky flows home.

On a flat stone, my father
lifts a slow gill, jackknife
glued with blood
and scales

for breakfast. This funny
finned suit and guts
I'll shovel into soil by a poplar
shivering dew.

Night not yet fully drained.

The fattest bass we skewer through the ass;
blacken its leopard-fast stripes over flames
to destroy all evidence
we ever awoke
to a north wind sniffing us.

Flaky flesh, tender
as sore human shoulders
from three days of oars.

The only witness:
a compact of words
shared like salt, a thermos
of green tea, all seasoned
with a little rain.

Ah, two henchmen and their dirty work.
Bones picking bones.
Fingers savoring tail and cheek meat.
A boy, a man. All morning

waves knock hard and hollow
a weed-wigged anchor
mermaids have raced gathering sailors' ears.

Something in the lake splashes:

a muscle, a bird,
a jewel

and no one home.

Mrs. Joseph B— on Love, Sin, & Celadon

When he came home from the war
we didn't sleep together for four months. He put
a sprinkler system in, ceiling moldings, chain-
sawed branches. I was touching myself

on the toilet and my daughter walked in. I grounded her
for mimicking the noises over dinner cabbage rolls.
How do you come back from that:
however many breaths like birds it torments him

he took from those people. He'd disappear
some evenings, so I picked up pottery and extra hours
at the travel agency. A man, a client, asked me to happy hour.
It was dark at 4:35; the snow airy wet, hypnotic.

We went to his condo after shrimp toast and I wanted to swallow
the ring in my purse. His wife, he said, had lesbian
inclinations he'd ignored at first. I listened to him,
his suffering over such preventable things, which, in a way,

is greater suffering, like a toothache versus soulless soul. He smelled
like smoke and cinnamon cologne and I thought he might be the Devil.
Still I went to him often. Did my husband even care?
I couldn't believe in ghosts, dead or living.

When I bloated with the other man's child, I confessed all.
My daughter screamed and wept; slammed the back door.
She called me slut, a traitor, and howled from the yard
how could I with a *the N-word*. I told her we're all human.

My husband didn't fight. We prayed and I killed my baby
at the same place I picketed with my Small Group
when I was my daughter's age. Sacrifice. An eye
for an eye. My husband killed

somewhere far away, and so did I, right here.
I knew it wouldn't resurrect his casualties. But I swear,
when seated each week with him hand in hand
in that fluorescent waiting room at the VA,

I understand his fear and longing to return to the desert.
He's a good man, and so wants to die.
It's why I married him.
And, now, why I must help him change.

Documentation

Everyone thought we were gay because we fought and talked trash and then made up like brothers sharing a prison cell in heaven. What to make of two young Asian men back then, suspect for arguing art and poetry, when the artist has long black hair and cheekbones like a bird of war? He read the first poem I ever showed anyone, said nothing, then a day later left Rilke on the kitchen table to slap common sense out of me, page by page. I was just beginning to feel how the last third of the alphabet is thicketed, more complex than the first and second—maybe as the last third of life is. He was dreaming in smoky pigments and for days would chase them, literally, splashing whole walls of abandoned warehouses to try to ignite some secret door to grace.

This month in Chicago, I went back to the fungal bar that bought our phony 19-year-old chop-socky accents, then watched the sun fall like a bloody egg. In a Koreatown that now feels underwater, I understood that only the dead finally belong to their bodies. The rest of us change, and that friction is the blessed pain.

And I promised, Kim, I'd write about you. A Thai stripper, much older, 25 or 26, with three other names depending on what you knew. Who loved musicals, Basquiat, Munch, but couldn't seem to decide between us two; finally picking some dude in a red BMW throbbing gangsta rap, and the flaws in our hearts were forever soldered brokenly together. She was lost like so many other pretty Asian girls here cut their own soft flesh with that exotic, double-edged sword—now barely a Vespa leaking blue smoke in a hot August wind.

The next year I tried my luck in Korea, teaching English, but this time when he and I met and wept it was over soju, not bourbon, and not for common disgrace, but a sighing sense of floating without having to swim. I found myself in the middle of the Taegu woman and him at a pojangmacha tent slurping rainy fishcakes. It was past dark, my interpretations slurred twofold, but for once I knew who I was and was not to myself.

We'd been searching for his biological mother for two weeks. All he had was one brittle mimeographed document with his name and age from the orphanage: Pak Tae-Young, four years old—which may or may not have been fiction.

The tiny, middle-aged Taegu woman wore pearl-pink rubber slippers and spoke with a bright urgency in her teary, wide-open eyes. I could barely keep up, her shigol dialect like flying a kite in a sandstorm. On the second meeting we visited her in her tiny apartment behind a middle school, where she boiled oxtail broth and cut vegetables in the kitchen. The social worker we were with got the Taegu woman's signature and informed her of the necessity of a blood test. We stayed behind, and drank milky makkoli rice wine seated on her yellow linoleum, until a voice began to thread my brain. When I went to the bathroom, I saw through a cracked door an older woman dressed in white, bowing repeatedly alone, weeping and muttering a gibberish as if the hoarse, bossy leader of a children's game. Later, I'd learn the tattooed lines on both the old mother and her grown daughter's wrists meant they'd been marked as mediums for the spirit world. Shamans. Or maybe just insane. It didn't matter. By then the blood tests came back 96% in the negative, and we knew reality better, but even less of the truth.

Three days before he was scheduled to go back to the States, another call came in from the classified ad we'd placed, and this time it was a man. They sat across from each other at the cafe, both chain-smoking, as the man recounted stories involving the ambulance he drove now that he was sober, and the fire that took his wife and house years before. I was surprised: he let the man twice reach hard, tobacco-tawny fingers forward and touch his nose.

The next afternoon, the man introduced us to his daughter, and by then I wasn't sure. By appearances they could have been siblings. I don't like to tell this story, because you don't want your people to look bad when already their names and history are blackened and charred, but at dinner that night the girl leaned over and informed me that her father had liver cancer and they needed seven hundred dollars. I laughed, but he didn't when I told him, and signed over the four hundred dollars he had in traveler's checks, surely knowing we'd never see the old man and girl again.

If the past is a rope to somewhere, it can also wrap your throat. He's dead twelve years and I don't think of him every day anymore, or the two apartments we shared, the kitten that for three years remained unnamed before running away, or the many words and whole episodes of that crazy Taegu woman and man's lives I now know I mistranslated. Others visit instead.

But I know he's there in my searching, and not just him, but that old woman in white muslin I glimpsed behind that cracked door, speaking her own kind of poetry so the spirits wouldn't be so lonely.

This morning I listened to birds talking to one another about a snake that had apparently entered the yard. The scrub jays inform the finches, who inform the squirrels and the jackrabbits, and so on, as maybe it's always been. And I dimly recalled a story he told me during the first week of our friendship. As we drifted off to sleep, spinning, I asked if he had any memories of the homeland, and he spoke something of his birth father, who he thought was a barber, dying suddenly of some illness, yes, and a beautiful mother who did all she could to keep him. There was a sister, though I can't remember if she was older or younger. And the wart on the back of his little hand, burned off when first he arrived in America; the scar of which he always carried like an amulet. . . . This part is true.

All the rest is what I was sent to interpret for you.

Genesis 4.0

In the beginning, there was a huge drop of milk.

—FULANI CREATION MYTH

The Latina hija in pink jumpsuit, silver-
bird earrings, & black pigtails, eyeballs
me in the Midtown Gobal Market food court
from her wooden highchair because I'm a strange Mexican

with my small eyes & loneliness larger than language.
Her thick-thighed, late-teens mother smiles & whispers
in her ear & it works for a minute. I'm free
to chew my food & memories

of other brown, some black, almost never white
kids perplexing over my own growing body
floating through years of similar hair,
lashes, tone . . . but what about his eyes? Again,

these corners & lids. The curious girl's
father is a brute of a superhero in a muscle shirt,
gunloaded arms garlanded with tattoos. I imagine
this young Mexican couple quickening the pulse

of birds outside their bedroom window; maybe
followed by a dream that one day a prince will guide

their child's hand to a brilliant altar before God; or even better,

a pen so their story can be secretly written

on the inner tag of His hem—

                       A myth of Bear & Tiger,

forced to live in a cave a hundred days, all humanity

at stake, nibbling only mugwort, or . . . anise? no,

tamarind, garlic, definitely not xalwo, maybe

yes, fenugreek? not salsa, cilantro,

sure, why not a dash of sriracha, cumin, a squeeze of lime?

Now the whole family, all four, has turned

to witness the injera cushioning my mouth,

their grins both embarrassed & proud

at their littlest one's giggle, blue bow, & mango lassi straw—

now aimed at the cross-eyed comic adult

made to recall his own

mother once leaning low:

Seung-won ah,

            finish your bab & just one more ghost.

Whorled

Dear speaker in a future age,
when only a handful of tongues remain
I write this to you as a song,
even as I know it won't do

Even as I know the words I speak are devastation
I don't expect you to understand
But I want you to know
there is another language in which I dream

Sometimes I think it's Korean
Other nights my dead halmoni sewing a broken room
Or my neighbors, a family of Ojibwas,
welding their minivan, cinder blocks teetering

Summer evenings the Hmong girl and boy echo hide
and seek with cousins down the street
Or, this spring, Juan, the Mexican kid next door,
suddenly fourteen, shuffling steps on the corner,

baggies stuffed in his shorts, truant every afternoon
I see him some days through my window, rapping in a back alley
alone in broken English to his iPod
As I've seen him since he was ten, youngest of four undocumented

brothers in a boarding room basement I watch
through their window well like an evening TV show
whose writers are all angry drunks
And I wonder what will happen to this slightly dumpy boy's

heart, out of sync with his tongue—the only two muscles
to move you with wings through this world
A shiny black SUV pulls up each Friday,
he climbs in, and I wonder

if I did the right thing three years back by urging my other
neighbor, an old white woman,
not to call the cops on him
Dear speaker in a future age,

when only a handful of lexical bouquets
remain to light these monstrous highways
I write this to you as a human
piece of coal

Origin of orange
Shelved away in some petrified repository
Even as I know it's too late for you to bind and open me
Even as I know yet another world language will become extinct this week,

forever gone, like Atlantis or Montezuma's Kingdom: Sumerian,
Gothic, Goguryeo, Tasmanian, Scots Gaelic, Mohawk, Iroquois—
like a global hurricane of power and indifference, veering
toward Flemmish and Basque, Ainu, Anishinabe, and, yes, one

day, if turnabout is fair play, maybe even this language I tease
apart for inconsistencies to house me
I wish I could tattoo this prayer to my palm,
even as I know it's way too long,

longer than my body, my whole life—this eviscerated
pink and black spilling
through the forest of my sleep
Maybe it's the colonial Japanese

screwed into a schoolboy, my father, who later
forced Russian on me—Otyets, wakarimaska?
Or the only three ideograms I remember of all
those my mother sat me before, fingers over hand,

ink brush two cold tons: *e sng one*
Though yesterday just another passionate Somali debate
awakening me on the 21A
A mismatched couple whispering

over borscht and piroshki at Kramarczuk's on Hennepin
Once some Greek harangue over the baklava's freshness at Bill's Imported
Ah yeah, and the phở tái every Sunday I supersize
whose bony broth brings tears to my eyes in Frogtown

And sometimes I know I'm just another ghost
passing through this century
One of a long line of hungry souls before me
Each a spiritual refugee

Dear father who art in heaven,
who fled your homeland, war torn, in flames,
I write this to you, Abonim, from the end of the world
to forgive you for your rage,

even as you emptied its fear
into your own family's tears—
to report: the view of Manhattan from the Williamsburg Bridge
        this summer is beautiful
All night, an entire island lit up, scintillating

like a Christmas tree asleep so peacefully on its side
Like the one Omoni crowned each December, a newborn prince
I relinquish you from the preterite
Spiritual RNA erased by missionaries and sunglassed generals

handing out candy, cigarettes, crosses, and European names
Dear Future, I'm writing you from an imperfect
case, in a secret code I've had to reinvent myself with
Associations and inflections

Rawest of imaginations
A Disciple of Time in a bulky patois adrift
Migrant with no motor, canvas, or oars
Only these few city stars—faulty neon thresholds

In truth, only two:
Dear *Time*, how I envy the cleanliness of your hands

Dear *Love*, why do I need your shadow so deeply inside mine?
I don't know where any of us is going,

but I'm sure on the other side of the world, there is a language I have never heard
It is beautiful, and in this dying tongue, there are words for Love and God
that resemble Bread and Wing
Or another forest language in which Mother and Knife

equal Drawer and Sing
And Island Wood is somewhere Desert Milk
And Berry, elsewhere is a Door
And if you added up all these dying words, and the people who speak them

All their memories, histories, and lessons
All their gods, jokes, rituals, and recipes
If you learned and stirred them, over and again, until
each utterance became a star, a new footprint, the marrow of a poem—

And yet, what do we say?
Not: *I am an incomplete dictionary*
But: *Go back to where you come from*
if you don't like it this way

And yet, in the canopy of listening, what rasps
in these voices is not hate, or even fear,
but grief
These groaning doors and shrinking portals to history

Dear speaker in a future age
when not six thousand or three thousand or even a dozen—
But only one origin of the world remains
I write this to you as an elegy

In the beginning, there was a word, but it got lonely
So it prayed for brothers, sisters, and neighbors, and yes,
love was born, but along with it came shame, passion, greed, more
love, benevolence, and need

And soon some of the words became flowers and trees
And others animals, and eventually some were human beings:
Queens and Workers,
Kings and

Thieves

Notes

Epigraph — *Old Boy* (2003) Jo-yung Hwan, Chun-hyeong Lim, Joon-hyung Lim, Chan-woo Park (screenplay), and Joon-hyung Lim (writer).

"Mourning in Altaic" — While writing this piece, I wrestled with the following: "People from different traditions should keep their own, rather than change. . . . In the United States [people] take something Hindu, something Buddhist, something, something. . . . That is not healthy. For individual practitioners, having one truth, one religion, is very important. Several truths, several religions, is contradictory." —DALAI LAMA

"Dream After Watching Nine Ozu Films One Weekend & Considering Imperial Japan's Response to the West's Colonization of 85% of the Pre-wwii World (Alone Over Beer & Falafel)" — Yasujiro Ozu (December 12, 1903–December 12, 1963)— silent-to-Technicolor film director whose distinctive, influential classics about family life throughout four decades of Japan's industrialization are often said to exemplify the concept of mono no aware, an acute awareness of the impermanence of things.

"Karaoke Poem" — C # / In the style of Dean Young + Issa + the Neptunes.

"Chosun 5.0" — Chosun, former name of Corea, currently known as South Korea and North Korea.

"Whorled" — Every two weeks, the final living speaker of a world language passes away. As with the extinction of a biological species, factors in language (and corresponding cultural) extinction involve the same political and economic engines that drive global pollution, deforestation, modern colonialism, and general destruction of biodiversity in all forms on the planet. Unlike "dead" languages such as Latin and Sanskrit, which evolved into other modern tongues and official and sacred functions, "extinct" languages, by definition, vanish, ultimately, in total along with their speakers' knowledges of cosmology, history, nature, health, psyche, myth, science, music, artistry, and ways of perceiving, thinking about, and assigning values within the world. Over the past 500 years, one half of the world's languages have disappeared. Of the roughly 6,000 languages spoken today, another half are predicted to become extinct after the next generation. On Wikipedia and elsewhere, the numbers are as acute as 90% language extinction by 2050.

ED BOK LEE was raised in South Korea, North
Dakota, and Minnesota. A former bartender, phys
ed instructor, journalist, and translator, he studied in
the U.S., South Korea, Kazakhstan, and Russia,
earning an MFA from Brown University. Lee has shared
his work in journals and anthologies, and on public
radio and MTV, and teaches part time at Metropolitan
State University in St. Paul. Lee's first book, *Real
Karaoke People,* was the winner of an Asian American
Literary Award (Members' Choice) and the PEN Open
Book Award.

COLOPHON

Whorled was designed at Coffee House Press, in the historic
Grain Belt Brewery's Bottling House near downtown Minneapolis.
The text is set in Kinesis.

FUNDER ACKNOWLEDGMENT

Coffee House Press is an independent nonprofit literary publisher. Our books are made possible through the generous support of grants and gifts from many foundations, corporate giving programs, state and federal support, and through donations from individuals who believe in the transformational power of literature. Coffee House Press receives major operating support from the Bush Foundation, the Jerome Foundation, the McKnight Foundation, from Target, and from the Minnesota State Arts Board, through an appropriation from the Minnesota State Legislature and from the National Endowment for the Arts. Coffee House also receives support from: three anonymous donors; Elmer L. and Eleanor J. Andersen Foundation; Around Town Literary Media Guides; Patricia Beithon; Bill Berkson; the James L. and Nancy J. Bildner Foundation; the E. Thomas Binger and Rebecca Rand Fund of The Minneapolis Foundation; the Patrick and Aimee Butler Family Foundation; the Buuck Family Foundation; Ruth and Bruce Dayton; Dorsey & Whitney, LLP; Fredrikson & Byron, P.A.; Sally French; Jennifer Haugh; Anselm Hollo and Jane Dalrymple-Hollo; Jeffrey Hom; Stephen and Isabel Keating; the Kenneth Koch Literary Estate; the Lenfestey Family Foundation; Ethan J. Litman; Mary McDermid; Sjur Midness and Briar Andresen; the Rehael Fund of the Minneapolis Foundation; Deborah Reynolds; Schwegman, Lundberg & Woessner, P.A.; John Sjoberg; David Smith; Mary Strand and Tom Fraser; Jeffrey Sugerman; Patricia Tilton; the Archie D. & Bertha H. Walker Foundation; Stu Wilson and Mel Barker; the Woessner Freeman Family Foundation; and many other generous individual donors.

To you and our many readers across the country,
we send our thanks for your continuing support.

Good books are brewing at www.coffeehousepress.org